The Unrelenting Burdens
of Gang Bangers

The Unrelenting Burdens of Gang Bangers

By:

Death Row Inmate,

Minister Kenneth D. Williams

Published by

Midnight Express Books
P. O. Box 69
Berryville, AR 72616
http://www.MidnightExpressBooks.com

The Unrelenting Burdens of Gang Bangers

Copyright ©2012 on the story by Minister Kenneth Williams

ISBN-13: 978-1530556205
ISBN-10: 1530556201

Published by

Midnight Express Books
P. O. Box 69
Berryville, AR 72616
http://www.MidnightExpressBooks.com

The Unrelenting Burdens of Gang Bangers

By:

Death Row Inmate,

Minister Kenneth D. Williams

Dedication

This work of grace and truth is dedicated to the memory of the Late Matthew Johnson. Your life was not in vain; your memory is not forgotten. What I couldn't understand back then...I clearly comprehend now.

Two small lights joined together in a dark place, give enough illumination to guide the lost to green valleys and still waters.

Series One

A wise man once said: "when the lord comes into our lives, first he lifts us, then he gifts us. Our gift is meant to lift other people."

It mesmerizes me profoundly that the sovereign God of the Universe has chosen to use my devious past as a tool to teach, strengthen, and restore to health the down trodden.

In 1989, I was lured into joining a street gang called "The Black Gangster Disciples" known also as the "Hoover's Folks". I was just 9 years old. My peers and I, all from low income, single parent homes, were seduced in by tall tales and dreaming big... Of things that would be enticing to young people, desperate to know their identity and where they fit in in this world. BGD, like all other gangs, gave an illusion of hope and serenity, a refuge from loneliness and vulnerability. It embraced me like a surrogate mother. It gave to me what I thought I needed, but never should have had.

Many undignified and disgraceful demands were made upon me, to prove my worthiness through discord and mayhem.

The Unrelenting Burdens of Gang Bangers

The more defiant I grew, the more popular and recognizable my name, "Pedy-Wee-Straw the devil's-son-in-law" became. It wasn't long before I found myself, at 10 years old, sentenced to the Arkansas Boys Reformatory in Pine Bluff.

It was like being sent to a resort for gang bangers, there were so many of us there.

Rehabilitation for delinquents in such a place was highly improbable, unlike character deterioration, which saturated the place.

The pathway my surrogate mother (the gang) directed me down was torturous. Where were the things I had been promised? Had I not held up my end of the bargain?

This wasn't what I expected at all. I wasn't being loved back, only used and abused mercilessly. Nevertheless, like any other unhealthy abusive relationship, I found myself unable to break away, even after my release from the reformatory school. No matter where I went, temptation and negative influence were always there. Consequently I spent my entire adolescence in and out of jail, until my graduation in 1996 from the juvenile system to that of the adult system, at the age of only sixteen.

"Many sorrows shall be to the wicked, but he who trusts in the Lord, mercy shall surround him." Psalm 32:10 NKJV

In the Arkansas Department of Corrections I discovered what I was running to was worse than what I was running from. I was instantly engulfed by the prison gang culture. I was one with chaos, an out-of-control product of my environment. What life had put in to me, I was determined to give it back with a vengeance.

Prisons are packed with teenage delinquents. Their down fall into obscurity and the reproach of society is their reckless decision to join a gang. If gang banging fails to put a person behind bars, six feet deep prematurely becomes an even higher possibility.

Ironically, even after suffering great loss of freedom, losing friends and family members to gang violence, most gang banger's loyalty to their gang remains unwavering. Should this be accredited to their steadfastness, or is it something else? I believe the latter.

"Don't you know that when you offer yourselves to someone, to obey him as slaves, you are

slaves to the one whom you obey." Romans 6:16

Young people are pledging allegiance to gangs without fully understanding what they are getting themselves into. After a person is initiated into a gang it's not always easy or safe to terminate membership. And then there's the dilemma with people wanting so much to see the best in what they have come to represent, they blind themselves to truth, seeing only lies.

The bible speaks about strongholds, which can dominate a person's mind, rendering them captive to distorted false beliefs; as the Apostle Paul wrote in 2 Corinthians 10:3-6

> *"For though we walk in the flesh, we do not war according to the flesh. For the weapons of our warfare are not carnal but mighty in God, for pulling down strongholds, ... "*

Once the mind is under subjection, the body does what it's told like a slave. Whose slave? Satan's.

After all, is he not the criminal minded architect behind the street gang epidemic that has a stronghold over gang members' minds and hearts? See the devil's credentials:

"The thief (Satan) does not come except to steal, kill, and to destroy." John 10:10

Street gangs are directly responsible for countless deaths and ruined lives. Take it from me, A former gang member, and now a death row prisoner who has lived the gangster life, shed innocent blood, moved up through the ranks, thinking I was making a name for myself. Gangs aren't worth a micro-second of your time.

Know yourself, your self worth, and competence. Gangs aren't worthy of you even on your lowest day.

Young people listen up. There are so many prestigious groups a person can associate and affiliate themselves with. You just have to get out there and look for them, for however long it takes. Parents, take the initiative and talk with your children about the danger of joining a gang. Encourage them to enroll in extra curriculum activities instead, such as sports and community service. These are productive and character building.

For my 15 years of gang banging, I have been rewarded with a solitary cell on death row, cut off from my family and the world. What a letdown! In spite of what has been my fate, in

5

this prison cell among the despised, I now have an intimate relationship with Jesus Christ whom is everything I need in life.

His reward adds no sorrow. Praise God for the Jailhouse visits! Rehab visits! Crack House visits! Etc.! Jesus makes at our request. His mercy, healing and deliverance are for all. He is the truth. He destroyed the stronghold of gang bondage in my life. I've become freer than I have ever been, and you can as well.

The Lord lifted me up, then he gifted me. A gift which I now use to help build others up with truth and enlightenment, so others will know to avoid the snare of gang involvement sat by Satan the devourer to destroy lives. Now that you know better, do better. Praise the Lord!

Series Two

Perhaps before you've heard something spoken, or read something written before, and its application left you arrested in development. I have. The quote, "The tears of a million mothers" left me fixated. What kind of dreadful act could cause such grief and hardship, as to make a million mothers cry tears of bitterness? To answer such a question, one only needs to look at what has made a million mothers shed tears: The loss of a child to gang violence and involvement.

It has been declared,

> *"A disobedient child shall not live half his days."* Ephesians 6:1-3.

Furthermore,

> *"A child left to himself brings shame to his mother."* Proverbs 29:15.

If these fallen tears could be bottled up, sent to Africa where there's drought in the land, the thirst of the people there would be sufficiently quenched. If mothers of the fallen, neglected to cry for their lost child in the streets, in prison, or in the grave as a result of gang activity, most likely, tears wouldn't be shed. One thing can be known for certain: Don't expect crocodile tears to come from the gang, for the gang can't comprehend nor express true love and compassion. To the spirit of a gang, its members are replaceable objects come a dime-a-dozen, courtesy of the gang's ability to manipulate, entice, and lure new recruits into its web of deterioration for devourment. Street Gangs can only give illusions of virtue and immortality to its members. What they can furnish and supply abundantly is death, tears, and destruction, clocked and wrapped nicely inside an enticing package. "Clearly the devil is in the details."

When considering the tears of mothers who have lost their children to gang violence, I think of the cause which provoked their tears. Mainly it's due, in large part, to the rebellious and out of control young folk, of which I was one, until I hit rock bottom on Arkansas Death Row.

The tears of my beloved mother were endless. It's the tears of despair, coming from mothers who are left picking up the pieces, they are the wages of sin and death for those bangers of gangs, these incorrigible delinquents, who love to push the envelope.

I've had to learn the hard way, such bitter tears aren't restricted to mothers, However, there's great hope for a man who possesses remorse for his indiscretions. Once he has seen clearly the irreparable destruction he has caused, the pain of it all can strike the heart of even the most hardened of gangsters. Apart from those who feel nothing, with hearts of stone, void of light. I speak from experience.

There must be a resolution to stopping these tears of bitterness and regret:

> "*The rod of correction imparts wisdom, but a child left to himself disgrace his mother...*" Verse 17 "*Discipline your son, and he will give you peace, he will bring delight to your soul.*" Proverbs 29:15, 17 NIV

> "*Train a child in the way he should go, and when he is old he will not turn from it.*" Proverbs 22:6 NIV

> "*And you, fathers, do not provoke your children to wrath, but bring them up in the training and admonition of the Lord,*" Ephesians 6:4 NKJV.

With exuberance let us not dare forget, although there are tears of despair, there are also tears of joy and happiness. Just take into account: what can make a million mothers cry tears of thanksgiving and gratitude? To answer such a question one only needs to examine what has caused such tears: Having a child who adherent to Exodus 20:12

> *"Children, honor your father and your mother,*
> *that your days may be long upon the land, which*
> *the Lord your God is giving you."* NKJV.

This is the first commandment with promise.

God blesses obedience. His word makes this assertion:

> *"The blessing of the Lord makes one rich, and*
> *he adds no sorrow with it."* Proverbs 10:22

No burdens.

Young people, if you're going to be the cause of your mother's tears, at least make those tears to be tears of joy, not of burden.

Series Three

"No servant can serve two masters; for either he will hate the one and love the other, or else he will be loyal to the one and despise the other."
Luke 16:13

My allegiance, like many others, laid with the "Black Gangster Disciples," and my loyalty and dedication were to King Larry Hoover, whom, ironically, I had never met. Hoover was the founder of BGD, which originated in Chicago, Illinois in the 70's, and spread across the Unites States, targeting predominately minority low income communities.

Like so many other youngsters in my neighborhood, I was swept up in the gang craze, that gave me the opportunity to wild out, for which I was commended. Our doctrinal philosophy was: "Money, Mack and Murder". As obedient servants/disciples, we obeyed without question.

We terrorized the city of Pine Bluff, Arkansas creating disorder. My peers and I were indoctrinated to believe we were somehow earning "stripes" or status within the gang. If we earned enough rank, we could then exercise control over others. To have such power and control over others proved to be a powerful motivator for me.

I was a disciple of King Larry Hoover. There could be no weakness in me. As Hoover's loyal disciple my obedience and conduct reflected upon him and, as we would say, upon the Gangster Disciple Nation.

We were to be a force to be reckoned with. Hoover's Disciples were to show no pity. Any and all weaknesses were to be eradicated. Being so dedicated and committed to our cause, members even prayed to this man – he who was not, nor is not, in heaven, but rather incarcerated within the United States penitentiary.

As a teenager I was diagnosed with a learning disability, and but somehow I was able to memorize the gangster prayer: "When I die, show me no pity, bury me deep in gangster city; place two pitch forks across my chest, tell King Hoover I did my best".

Having our conscience darkened, we prayed to and worshipped this man, totally ignorant of God's commandment. Jesus said to him:

"Away from me, Satan, For it is written; worship the Lord your God, and serve him only." Matthew 4:10. NKJV

Worshipping another man is indeed sinful. This one act of defiance to God subjects all who engage in such conduct, to enslavement. Not so much as to enslavement to Hoover's rule, he's but a man. But to someone far sinister...

It is so written:

"Most assuredly, I say to you, whoever commits sin is a slave of sin." John 8:34.

Furthermore,

"Don't you know that when you offer yourselves to someone to obey him as slaves, you are slaves to the one whom you obey." Romans 6:16

If an individual is involved in a street gang, he or she is blindly being misled by the persons leading. An essential question needs to be asked, and answered: Who or what backs the Leader who is leading the followers? Understand this: Our leaders can be mislead, lied to, and victimized just like their followers.

"He who is not with me (God) is against me, and he who does not gather with me scatters abroad." Matthew 12:30

Let us not be so blinded by Satan that we cannot see, which side of the aisle of good and evil gangs are on. Actions have always spoken louder than words. If a person is gang involved, make no mistake about it, they're against God even if they deceive themselves into believing otherwise. "You can't serve two masters." It is written.

And so is the fate of Satan and all his disciples:

"But the wicked shall perish; and the enemies of the Lord, like the splendor of the meadows, shall vanish. Into smoke they shall vanish away." Psalm 37:20

I, Kenneth D. Williams, am no longer a disciple of King Larry Hoover, nor of Satan's, but I am a disciple of the King of Kings, the Lord of Lords and Savior, Jesus Christ. My loyalty and allegiance is to him alone, who will not abandon my soul to the grave, but will raise me and all others who trust and believe in him to eternal life. I've joyfully put down my black flag, for the cross, and encourage others to put down their gang colors, whether it be red, blue, black, or gold; the cross is for you, never against you.

The Unrelenting Burdens of Gang Bangers

Series Four

In retrospect…looking back on my 31 years of life, I've blown some amazing opportunities, as well as ruined priceless friendships, due to my notorious gang affiliation. Other things of importance, including family, often took back seat when it came to banging; thus being my position, I paid a heavy price.

Be certain, that the fate of gang members is a perilous one. It will be a wasted life ending in a wheelchair, in prison, or in an early grave. That can't be emphasized enough.

If a poor, uneducated man, or an illegal immigrant has few opportunities, a living or dead gangster has even fewer. Better yet, a dead gangster has no opportunities.

> *"…But the dead know nothing and they have no more reward, for the memory of them is forgotten."* Ecclesiastes 9:5.NKJV

If it can be said, the dead may obtain peace of mind; that peace has to be found in not having to live with the burdens of a wasted life. Contrarily, prisoners incarcerated for gang related crimes, will struggle periodically with such burdens. When opportunity came knocking, I either gave myself permission not to answer, was distracted with lesser important things, or sometimes I just didn't care. In my ignorance, I allowed myself to believe the opportunities which did come my way, they would always be there for me. Wrong! Opportunities aren't required to stick around waiting on anyone. There are too many other people just waiting on their big break.

Just one felony conviction on your record is sufficient reason to disqualify you from certain employment, from obtaining a desired security clearance, applying for certain grants, joining the military, serving in law enforcement, etc...

Gang banging has unforeseeable consequences and can cause irreplaceable, irreconcilable damages. It burns bridges opposed to building them for people to walk across to the city of opportunity and privilege.

During the commission of a criminal offence, gang bangers often believe his or her actions are acceptable, permissible, somehow cool or even necessary; such a belief surely would twist a person's logic. One needs to consider in advance: Will this action promote me in a worthy manner, wherefore no repercussion will manifest? Will I be deprived of my freedom if I commit this act? A wise man always weighs and considers his next move, while a fool moves without taking anything into account. Had I applied these principles, I most certainly wouldn't have blown opportunities, I would have firmly secured the ones I had, and even drawn in others.

Gang bangers are infamously known for their tattoos, displayed gang signs covering their arms, chest, neck, and maybe the worst place to have a gang related tattoo, on the face. The person who conceived the tear drop tattoo, usually tatted underneath a person's eye, indicating he or she murdered someone obviously gave no thought to ever attending a job interview.

In such a case, job discrimination, understandingly, doesn't apply. No employer is likely to give someone a job who has a tear drop tattooed on their face, or any other gang related sign visibly on display. Surely this would harm business, and so would sagging pants, worn the way gangsters like to wear them: Low.

Good things seem to avoid bangers, while bad things seek them out. People of statue and of integrity keep their distance from gang bangers. If you've ever been a gang banger, maybe you've seen it before: You were walking up the street, someone else was coming down it; upon seeing you they cross to the other side to avoid you. You walk by a parked car, the person inside notices you, and without hesitation they lock the doors as if you're an unclean and impure subject. On occasion I found myself angered behind certain people's response to my presence. Mostly noted, when I was a teenager, parents openly rebuked their son(s) for associating with me. They would say "That little boy is bad, he's a gang member and I don't want you hanging with him. He's trouble." An inconvenient truth, they were right. "Do you not know that a little leaven leavens the whole lump?"

> *"Do not be misled: Bad company corrupts good character."* 1 Corinthians 15:33

It only takes a change of heart and association to no longer be the black sheep. Parents harbor no ill will toward well-behaved kids playing with their kids; it's the black sheep they find detestable. Although I desired to have friendships with some normal boys and girls, I eventually counted the loss of having such friendships a small price to pay for a life-style of being a gangster. Consequently, I foolishly handed my childhood and all of its glories over to oppression. From then on, until I asked Jesus Christ to be my Lord and Savior on May 9, 2005, I carried a burden you would find extremely hard to bare.

No natural man can survive what I've endured in life without the divine intervention of God.

More times than I care to remember, I've had guns drawn down on me from both criminals and police alike. At any time I could have been shot, killed or crippled. Although I've been shot at from every direction, thanks to the grace of the Almighty God, and to the people who did not cease praying for me, I've never been shot. This is a rare luxury for gang bangers.

I joyfully declare, I missed that bullet, but unfortunately, I didn't miss the other bullet...

Being a gang banger, if you live long enough, and in some cases time is no factor - you will either end up being shot or killed; or, like me, you'll end up killing someone else. What an unnecessary burden to have to live with.

The Unrelenting Burdens of Gang Bangers

Series Five

"They are blind leaders of the blind. And if the blind leads the blind, both will fall into a ditch."
Matthew 15:14

In June of 1998, I was asked to do something most saddened, which I'd never been called upon to do before. The request so caught me by surprise, totally unprepared. But then again, who is ever prepared to bury a loved one. I was asked to be a pall bearer for the late Matthew Johnson, a 13 year old boy who had accidently shot himself in the head while playing with a loaded gun he never should have had. But you know how it is with gang bangers, they're intoxicated by the tough boy mentality and reputation.

Pistol packing stimulates the masculine ego. Having an equalizer can make a man feel invisible, when he's not.

Young Matthew found out the hard way he's not made out of air, but flesh, bone, and blood; his lack of knowledge and underestimating the danger of a gun cost him his life.

Matthew and I were homies, brothers of what we called "The struggle". We grew up in the same gang-infested neighborhood; we both lived as outlaws who ran the streets of Pine Bluff, Arkansas, living dangerously on the edge. There was an age difference between us: when he was 13, I was 19. He was my apprentice, influenced in like-manner as I had been influenced by other older gang bangers.

We were also bonded through a relationship I had with his sister Demetria. Matthew was the uncle to my daughter. Right before Matthew's death, he lived with Demetria when it was safe to do so. He had run off from his foster home and found shelter there.

He no longer attended school, fearing apprehension. The juvenile court had ordered the police to pick him up, therefore he went on the run.

Most of Matthews's time was spent on the streets where he made his hustle. He burglarized people's homes and cars, which is where he most likely came into possession of the weapon used in ending his life.

He, along with other delinquents, was kicking up so much dust, his sister Demetria grew very concerned about him. She expressed these concerns to me, feeling that I could somehow pull his coat tail.

During one of my visits to pick up my daughter, Matthew asked if he could ride along. Seizing the opportunity to converse with him, we turned a few corners during which I encouraged him to slow his roll some. I completely understood the dilemma Matthew was in. His life was a repeat of mine. Staring into his life was like looking into a mirror. I was ten years old the first time I was sentenced to a boy's school for reform. After my release, I committed recidivism over and over again. I fled just about every foster home my case worker placed me in.

At sixteen years old I was sentenced to prison for first degree escape from "The Arkansas Serious Offenders Program" and for second degree battery. I received two five-year sentences to be run concurrent. After serving two years and two months, I was released on April 2, 1998, under parole supervision.

Just by having Matthew in the car with me, knowing the police were searching for him, this violated my parole conditions.

I felt as if there was only so much I could tell Matthew concerning his behavior. I had no desire to come across as a hypocrite. My life's choices were far more toxic than his.

I spared him the "Do as I say, not as I do," speech. For the most part, young people end up doing the exact opposite: They do as you do, not what you say. But still, I felt obligated to tell him, "Pull back some". If anyone knew of the dangers he faced living the way he was, that someone was me.

In hindsight, now that I look back, I might have told him enough to satisfy my conscious. To say I did something. And although we always say we could have done more, I could have done much more to deter him from his reckless decision making. Had I done so, perhaps his fate could have been altered.

It pains me to say, I and others came up short in the role model category. Notwithstanding, we more than contributed in the "Dropping-The-Ball" department, and no amount of tears I can shed now will change that!

If only this was an isolated case, perhaps it would be more bearable; regrettably, it's not. People all around the world struggle with the premature loss of a love one. And, like myself, they find themselves asking the questions: "Couldn't I have done more?" "Why didn't I do more?" The guilt of an inadequate performance can be a deal breaker, if not dealt with appropriately.

No thanks to my inaction, I had to look upon the stiff, cold face of Matthew at his funeral. As my eyes were fixated upon his lifeless body in utter disbelief, my ears were filled with the cries of grief which came from those whom loved him. He seemed at peace in his casket, a peace which eluded him in life.

He was only thirteen years old when his life was snuffed out. By his own hand the blow of death struck him. That very same hand had thrown up the "Pitch Fork" which represented Gangster Disciple. That hand had greeted me in the manner gang members shake hands. That hand had been used to hold marijuana blunts up to his mouth and beers. That hand was now resting neatly at his side, where it could no longer harm him.

The mourners who participated in Matthew's funeral did not attend because Matthew was a gangster, but because he was family and a friend of the mourners. And if, without my knowledge, someone did attend his funeral to pay their respects just because he was a gang member, their presence was so small they went unnoticed in a city like Pine Bluff, AR, where there's no shortage of gang bangers.

A funeral is the last time to pay final respect to the person who has died. Any true friend would attend, and yet Matthew's gang family... who pretended to care so much for him was missing in action. Let this be a sign to all gang members.

I found myself confused and angry behind Matthew's death. I couldn't understand why he had died at such a young age, yet not me. My life of crime started way earlier than his, plus I was three times as reckless and rebellious as he was. However, I was the one standing in front of his casket staring down on him. By all reason and logic, the order of death should have been reversed. Tears should have filled his eyes as he stood over me in my casket. He should have been one of my pall bearers. This enigma evaded me for quite some time. Only now does it become clear to me: God has a calling on my life to minister his word and to tell of his goodness, his grace, salvation, and mercy.

Perhaps you heard it said: "The devil meant it for evil, but God turned it around for my good." What I have discovered is God has given me a story very dear to my heart, one I can draw experience and wisdom from in order to teach others of the dangers of not warning a brother when you see him headed over a cliff. We are commanded by God to love one another. Love always tells the truth, it's never selfish; it casts out fear which holds people back from telling others how it is.

Periodically we confess we love somebody; but, is it true love that we have for one another, or is it some other feeling or emotion masquerading inside of us appearing as love? If I truly loved Matthew in the manner that God's word describes love in 1 Corinthians 13:4:8:

> *"Love is patient, love is kind. It does not envy, it does not boast, it is not proud. It does not dishonor others, it is not self-seeking, it is not easily angered, it keeps no record of wrongs. Love does not delight in evil but rejoices with the truth. It always protects, always trusts, always hopes, always perseveres. Love never fails. But where there are prophecies, they will cease; where there are tongues, they will be stilled; where there is knowledge, it will pass away."*

My conversation with Matthew would not have been what it was. It would have been more direct, compassionate; there would have been follow ups, which came after the intervention.

> *"And above all things have fervent love for another, for love will cover a multitude of sins."*
> 1 Peter 4:8

This is what authentic love looks like, and if you don't find a similar pattern then you must not have love for your brother - but rather something else, which could end up costing you dearly.

My young apprentice, whom I blindly led astray, is dead. As for me, I'm on Death Row, the closest a person can come to being in a grave without actually being there. Given the way Matthew and I lived our lives, gang banging, was this not to be expected?

I walked in darkness, I lived wickedly; Matthew followed. Easily as we did so, we could have been children of the light who walked in righteousness. I don't claim to have had no choice in how I lived my life. Quite the contrary, we all have free will and will be rightfully held accountable for our actions, or inactions by All Mighty God on the day of judgment: Acts 17:31.

Enticement and negative influences are two powerful forces unleashed upon us all to destroy us; nonetheless, they can be effectively resisted. The case I want to make is that not everyone who grows up in the projects, the hood, the ghetto, join a gang. Therefore no excuses, there's enough blame to go all around for this gang mess we're in.

Adolescents themselves are partially to blame if they join a gang. Gang recruiters share in the blame. So do parents who neglect to properly supervise and discipline their children. The police are to blame for not caring enough to crack down on gangs in minority communities. Politicians are to blame for their lack of management with this problem. For not adequately funding gang prevention programs, neglecting a hands-on approach, all of which suggest this problem hasn't been a top priority to them.

Finally, a lot of preachers aren't speaking out enough against gang involvement. They'd rather preach pleasant non-offensive sermons from the safety of their pulpits, when they should be out on the corners, in front of crack, weed, and gambling houses warning those walking in darkness, of the coming judgment if they don't repent of their sinful ways.

We've all dropped the ball in some way, and boy does it show unmistakably in our school houses, in our jails, and prisons, our rehabs, and yes...most regrettably, our graveyards, too. No sir, Matthew and I aren't alone. We're not the only ones who've paid a hefty price. The gang epidemic, that has declared war on humanity, can no longer be ignored or left unchecked. Like a cancer, it won't "just go away" but will consume all the good around it, leaving only death and destruction behind. Only if people begin to set aside their indifference will this gang epidemic be put into check.

Writing about Matthew's life along with my own, telling of the dangers of gang involvement for others to read it and hopefully share what they have learned with others, this is an effective and creative step towards combating our common enemy that has its ugly claws wrapped around the necks of so many they can't be counted.

It's highly unique of God to strategically use a former gang member such as myself, to connect, resonate, enrich, and liberate the hearts of gangsters. The Lord revolutionized my life, utilized the knowledge, resources, and standing I have with gang members to reason with them through my writings. He seeks to communicate with all who have an ear to listen and a heart to obey.

There's no better time for me to share this verse than right now:

> *"For you see your calling, brethren, that not many wise according to the flesh, not many mighty, not many noble, are called. But God has chosen the foolish things of the world to put to*

shame the wise, and God has chosen the weak things of the world to put to shame the things which are mighty; and the base things of the world and the things which are despised God has chosen, and the things which are not, to bring to nothing the things that are, that no flesh should glory in His presence." 1 Corinthians 1:26-29

You see, God's grace is sufficient enough to turn anyone's life around, no matter what sinister or diabolical thing they may have done. He's still able to use us. I am a living witness, much like the Gadarene demoniac, a man Jesus delivered from demon possession in Luke 8:27.

The only matter which needs to be resolved, will you allow yourself to be used by God? Where does your allegiance lie? In the kingdom of light or in the kingdom of darkness? No one can serve two masters. I chose the light; I am no longer blind, but now I see. Permit me to lead you out of bondage, out the darkness to Jesus Christ…who is "The Way, The Truth, and The Life," John 14:6

The Unrelenting Burdens of Gang Bangers

N.O.G.

Neutral of Gangs Questionnaire

A list of questions has been prepared to test your beliefs regarding gangs. To reprove any false doctrine and to encourage a better and clearer understanding of the challenges we face as a society dealing with gangs and their impact on communities.

It is preferable that you work out your answers on a sheet of paper. Upon completion of the test, share your answers with an adult, a mentor; someone you're comfortable with who can offer sound advice with objectivity.

N.O.G. Questionnaire

1. Are you a gang member? If you answered yes, what gang do you represent?

2. Why do you feel it's OK to be a gang member?

3. Is a person more or less likely to suffer loss…as a gang member?

4. What's the life span of a gang member? See Proverbs 10:27.

5. Why would the parents of gang members ever be proud of them?

6. Explain why jailhouses, prisons, and grave yards are so occupied with gang members?

7. How many successful gang members do you know? If any, why are they so few in numbers?

8. Can you think of a single reason the world wouldn't be better off without gangs?

9. While gang violence has resulted in the termination of countless lives, in what instance are you aware of where lives were preserved by a gang?

10. What role, if any, are you willing to take in your community to oppose gang violence? What is hindering you from fulfilling it?

11. How have you personally been affected by the dangers of gang violence?

12. Where is the wisdom found in joining a group where you must first be handled roughly with brutality, and in some instances, be degraded before you can become a

member?

13. In terms of virtuality, what's a gang to offer you that can't be obtained outside a gang?

14. What words of wisdom can you ascribe a grieving parent who has lost a child to gang violence?

15. Imagine yourself as a deceased gang member. You lost your life in a gang fight. You've been given the chance to travel back to speak with yourself before you were killed. What advice would you give yourself? Why would it make a difference towards changing your fate? If you are a gang member, why not now give yourself that advice and pray it makes a difference.

16. Someday you might be a parent, if you are not already. If your kid comes to you and asks for your approval to join a gang, would he or she have it? Why or why not?

17. Most gang members are between the ages of 16 and 30. Older people, in large, are not gang affiliated. Why do you think this is? Could it be that older, more experienced people are wiser? Explain your answer.

18. What do you want your legacy to be? Should it reflect

light or darkness? If you answered light, how can gang banging be brought into agreement with Light? See Proverbs 22:1.

19. Gang members often strive over their indifferences. It's also true they actually have more things in common. If then they fight over indifferences, and even the things they have in common don't deter their hunger for violence, how then are gangsters not engineered for self-destruction?

20. According to the scriptures, who is the real architect behind the street gang epidemic? See Ephesians 6:12; John 10:10

21. No retirement benefits are given to gang members. No monthly pay check in the mail, no insurance, no dental care. Not even a going away party for their service, If they receive nothing worthy, how then can they dispute the claim: "It all was for nothing"?

Here are a few multiple choice questions. Circle either yes or no for the correct answer.

1. Do you think God approves of gang violence and affiliation?

    ___ Yes   ___ No

    See Isaiah 55:7; Proverbs 24:21-22

2. Do you think Satan, the Devil, would approve of gang violence and affiliation?

    ___Yes   ___No

    See John 10:10

3. Does gang involvement breed and encourage disobedience?

    ___Yes   ___No

    See Proverbs 29:16

4. Do you agree that known gang members are likely to receive a good job or admission to an ivy league university?

    ___Yes   ___No

    See Proverbs 13:21

5. Would you be willing to support stronger, more creative anti-gang legislation and incentives aimed at curbing gang violence?

   ___Yes   ___No

See Psalms 94:16

6. If you were to witness a gang-related crime, or learn of one committed by someone, would you be courageous enough to speak up?

   ___Yes   ___No

See Ephesians 5:11

7. Gang members are known for their heated exchanges over colors of clothing and other wear, and over territory. Are these baseless and insignificant things ever worth the fuss? Worth the bloodshed?

   ___Yes   ___No

See Proverbs 20:3

8. Perhaps you heard of the Hall of Fame for deceased gang Leaders. If you haven't, don't worry; there isn't one. Have any of the gang leaders, dead or alive, ever been recognized as a national hero?

___Yes   ___No

See Psalms 9:5

9. Does the Bible teach that gang members go to Heaven after they die?

___Yes   ___No

See Psalms 92:7; Proverbs 11:21

10. The war against ending gang violence and affiliation. Is it winnable, containable, or treatable?

___Yes   ___No

As a society, are we winning or losing this war?

___Yes, for winning   ___No, for losing

Shouldn't you be helping either way if you truly care?

___Yes   ___No

See Romans 12:21

The Unrelenting Burdens of Gang Bangers

Gangs' Modus Operandi "The Blue Print"

For gangs to survive it's absolutely necessary that they acquire a steady flow of new recruits, as well as maintain sufficient numbers in their ranks. Their effectiveness is contingent upon their numbers and how wide spread the gang can become.

Membership is the lifeline of any gang, group or clique. Without it gangs are ineffective. Indeed, there is strength in numbers, even for wrongdoers.

What would be the fate of a gang if its lifeline was severed? It would die. A street gang's success means society has lost the advantage. In order to reverse matters, society must gain the advantage. The advantage goes to the opponent best prepared, equipped, who knows and understands the strengths and weaknesses of the other.

This written assessment endeavors to uncover the gang's modus operandi, show how it's put into effect, and lay out an effective counter plan aimed at disarming a street gang's effectiveness. In turn, this will strengthen communities.

I offer this assessment based on personal experience as a former member of the "Black Gangster Disciples" for fifteen years in the city of Pine Bluff, Arkansas.

STEP ONE: ACQUIRE A TARGET

Gangs specifically target certain types of people, certain class of people, believing they are easy pickings. They are the poor, and uneducated and those who are without guidance and direction. These include children who are orphaned by death or abandoned by one or both parents; runaways, delinquents, and/or those susceptible to crime and violence. Gangs radar in on them like a bat on a juicy bug. They are the ones of least resistance. They are sheep separated from the flock, defenseless, "as opposed to the more grounded, wholesome types." Gangs have nothing to offer them, so they are largely ignored for the lost, lonely and often unloved outsider.

STEP TWO: ENTICE

When it comes to recruitment techniques, colleges are masters of the game. They flaunt their big names and reputation around the amount of higher degrees they offer, and their state of the art facilities. Higher education helps to secure a profession leading to a higher standard of living, and of course, they all claim to have the greatest facility. Unlike the institutions of higher learning, an organization lacking in the prestige department, such as a gang, uses a different standard to draw the potential recruit's interest.

Mankind has a natural lust for power and position. History has shown this to be true over and over again, going back to the Garden of Eden. Thus gangs are selling and marketing to the youth things like position in the gang to rule and power to corrupt.

Ranking gang members are granted certain privileges and certain pleasures. Imagine what this does to the ego. For those ill-equipped to resist, the temptation proves to be more than they can bear.

STEP THREE: INDOCTRINATION

As ruthless outlaws, the street gang passionately seeks to claim both a person's mind and body, to assert control, and influence prospective recruits' minds. The gang propagates their propaganda through creeds, laws, memorandums and through signs and symbols. This gives the gang an appearance of organization, love, unity, structure and intelligence which are things to covet and admire.

The words love, life, loyalty, wisdom, knowledge and understanding can be found in gang literature. These words are merely fronts for a deeper darkness wishing to shun suspicion. The gang's true agenda only becomes known after it's too late, after the hooks are in. Seeing value where there really isn't any has been the perfect snare for many.

STEP FOUR: TAKE OWNERSHIP

A wise man wrote that a man is a slave to whatever masters him. Once a gang has its tentacles impelled in its prey, the prey is rendered powerless. The gang's tentacles are its doctrines, being sunken into hearts and minds.

Food consumed by a person enters the digestive system through the stomach where it's broken down, soon to become a part of the person. In a like manner, once joined with a gang, that person becomes one with it. After they have been consumed, they're broken down.

African American slaves in the 1700s through the 1800s were recognized on record by carrying their master's name. To protect their "property", slave owners would sometimes brand or cut marks into the bodies of their slaves. These brands and marks, like the brands on cattle, horses or hogs were registered to the owner.

Gang members are identified by their "owner's" name, Crip...Gangster..., etc. and are branded with gang tattoos and gang markings in the flesh that declare they are owned. They are someone's stuff.

STEP FIVE: RELEASE THE WOLVES

The gang's foot soldiers (wolves) are at the bottom of the pack. They are sent out to stir up trouble, to create fear and chaos, which translate to power and street creds. When people in the community fear street gangs, they bow down to them. The street gang operates its criminal enterprise freely, without threat from people within the community. Fear and chaos are a gang's bread and meat, without them, they don't eat. Therefore, the wolves must be dispatched if the gang is to survive. A friendly street gang can't rightly be called a street gang.

These wolves also serve to protect territories, spread the gang's influence, and recruit others.

The Unrelenting Burdens of Gang Bangers

Discussion Points
Gangs' Modus Operandi

1. How and in what manner is a street gang's success society's loss?

2. What are the common factors shared by street gangs and recruits?

3. What recruitment techniques have you observed or experienced?

4. What human needs do gangs claim to fulfill? (Note to facilitator: Discuss Maslow's Theory concerning the hierarchy of needs).

5. What part does ego play in your decision making?

6. What is your personal "creed"?

7. The word "slavery" has different meanings to different people. What is the dictionary definition of slavery? How does that differ from yours?

8. How can you take ownership of yourself?

The Counter Plan To Gangs' Modus Operandi "The Blue Print"

STEP ONE: An Evasive Target

With gangs targeting particular types of people, it only makes sense to be informed of who these types are and why they're targeted.

The company we keep can place us at risk of being targeted.

Benjamin Franklin said, "He who lies with dogs gets up with fleas." We're no better than the company we choose to keep. Certain company draws certain attention. If you surround yourself with riff raff, you may not be riff raff, but you will be perceived as such and perception is reality.

The places we choose to hang out can make us targets. Remember the adage, "Birds of a feather flock together." Places like clubs, bars, certain city parks where thugs hang, are all risky places. Jails, rehabs, prisons and the streets are all places that make the list. Certain alternative schools and areas of hang out in public schools are also hot zones where gangs operate. Nothing good happens after midnight.

Avoiding these places if you can or being vigilant in them if you can't avoid them will make a person less of a target.

Just as the lioness in heat signals her readiness to mate to any available male thru her body language, our body language will send messages. Street gangs are quite savvy at reading body language, i.e., a kid acting tough, as if he's "down", a kid wearing sagging pants, the type and manner in which a hat is worn. Even the colors of clothing, down to the brand can send messages intentionally or unintentionally.

Being more aware of your appearance and how you're perceived, make a huge difference. Making the necessary adjustments makes a person less of a target for gangs.

STEP TWO: Don't Be Enticed

To be enticed is to be artfully attracted by arousing hope or desire. It is a temptation, a lure into a trap. To avoid this entrapment, a person needs morals and values to anchor them and keep them from drifting off into dangerous waters. Having sound morals gives you standards in your behavior and conduct. No matter what's put before you to lure you away, you would be hard pressed to be uprooted from an established foundation. The gang's attempt to persuade you becomes nearly impossible.

Remember this: There is nothing that a gang can offer you that cannot be snatched away in the blink of an eye.

STEP THREE: Sound Doctrine

Your best defense against street gang's false, fake and harmful doctrine is to equip yourself with a sound doctrine. Possessing good and sound doctrine can enlighten, empower and protect you. The informed are best prepared to stand against opposition and prevail. They are able to defend what they believe without wavering in doubt or uncertainty. Those who are uninformed or misinformed stand to suffer great loss and be lead astray by whatever deceives them.

A sound doctrine is your strength against the street gangs' indoctrination. It is the mental defense of your mind, protecting you from the lies and falsehood of the street gang.

STEP FOUR: Freedom Over Bondage

Gangs do not offer true freedom to anyone-only an illusion of freedom. Freedom is not found in gangs because gangs are synonymous with lawlessness and discord. Breaking the law, of course, can result in punishment which can lead to incarceration and loss of freedom.

The face of a gang may appear to smile with freedom. But beware. Behind those smiling lips are vicious teeth that cut like shackles slicing into bare ankle flesh.

A person doesn't run to gangs for freedom and happiness. They run from them to find it. They avoid gangs to hold on to their freedom. They dare not believe all the lies and propaganda gangs sell to lure people into their net of bondage.

STEP FIVE: Don't Be Wolf Bait

The best protection against becoming wolf bait (gang bait) is to take preventative action. This action includes awareness of the dangers. Assuredly, just as awareness is strength, unawareness is a disadvantage and weakness.

Vicious wolves do not focus on the strong able body prey, but upon the weak and feeble. To avoid becoming bait, one mustn't frequent the wolves' hunting grounds such as bars and clubs, in high crime areas and known gang territories.

Discussion Points
The Counter Plan

1. What does it mean "He who lies with dogs gets up with fleas"?

2. What is meant by ''Perception is reality"?

3. What does "Birds of a feather flock together" mean?

4. What does "Nothing good happens after midnight" mean?

5. What does it mean to be "Down"?

6. What kind of signals or messages do you want to send?

7. What are your moral values? Would you hide someone from the police? Would you help cover up a murder? Would you lie in court or to the police to protect someone? Anyone?

8. Where are the local gang territories in your city? How do they mark their territories?

Tell Tale Signs That Your Child Might Be Gang Related

Being unaware of the status of a child is detrimental to the child's well being. Children conceal way too much and parents are missing even more. Parents are often distracted by lesser important things to the point they're missing signs, even those out in the open.

My mother found out I was gang related only after my brother, who wasn't too pleased that I was following in his destructive footsteps, had to tell her. The signs were there all along yet, she missed them. Mama just did not know what to look for. Here are a few signs your child has fallen prey to a street gang:

1. Tattoos: Although not exclusive to gang members, tattoos can be a sign of affiliation with a street gang. So let's look at what distinguishes gang tattoos from others; Hand signs and symbols; to Gangster Disciples, the six point star represents their gang. The five-point star represents the Vice Lord gang. The double lightning bolt tattoo represents the Aryan Nation Brotherhood. Some gang tattoos even

spell out their gang name. These are only a few examples. To be able to view these signs and symbols you must Google them under gang signs, symbols and tattoos.

2. Hand stacking: A gesture gang members do with their hands, fingers and arms. It's a performance through which signs are "Thrown Up" with the intent to promote certain things about the gang, certain beliefs and practices. Some of these gestures have been constructed to disrespect other gangs. If your kid has been observed stacking, this is sufficient cause for you to be alarmed. Intervention is required immediately.

3. Violent Behavior: Young people who join gangs will sooner or later feel pressured to conform to the image of a gangster; being notorious. They act out in school and in the neighborhood, beating up other children with the help of others. These are characteristics of a little gang banger or one in the making.

4. Hanging Out With Known Gang Members: This is a strong indication your child has joined a gang. But if he or she hasn't, it's only a matter of time. It rarely means anything else. Why risk even being wrong by allowing the temptation to continue? Put a stop to it now!

5. Dress Code: Biker gang members wear a vest with the name of their gang on it: "Hells Angels". Street gang members wear their hats toward a certain direction. Example: Gangster Disciples wear theirs toward the right, Vice Lords wear theirs toward the left. The Crips and Bloods are no different. Street gangs identify by what color clothes they wear: Bloods wear red. Crips wear blue. Gangsters wear black and Vice Lords wear gold. The handkerchief worn on the head or "Dew Rag" in the above colors is often used for a flag identifying a gang. Saggy pants or sagging and the "hip hop" style clothing are all gang inspired. Take notice of these tell tale signs.

6. Idolizing Gangster Characters in Film and in Music: We accept into our hearts those things we like. They appeal to us on some level. We even fantasize about being certain characters that inspire us. We're not immune to negative influences which fascinate us. Fantasy can become our reality if we fail to protect ourselves.

7. Graffiti: In gang territories graffiti on structures is as plentiful as bullet holes in stop signs. It's on bridges, vacant houses, street signs, etc. Graffiti is one way gangs mark their turf with their signs to warn rival gangs to stay clear.

Not every tagger who paints graffiti is gang-related, but everyone gang related has painted, sprayed or drawn in chalk, gang graffiti. Be aware of signs around you. It just might be your child doing the graffiti. The basic rule for dealing with graffiti is 3 R's; Report, Record, Remove. Report the graffiti on your property to the police. It is vandalism. Record by photographing the graffiti. Then remove by washing it off or painting over the graffiti.

8. The Language of Gangs: Listen closely to what your child is saying and how he or she says it. Conversations in person, on the telephone or through social media can tell you what they might not want you to know. For example: Crips address each other as "Cuz". Bloods refer to each other as "Dog". Gangsters will ask "What's up Kinfolk" or "What's up Gangster". Vice Lords will ask "What's up Lord". These greetings are dead giveaways that a street gang is exerting influence over your child.

9. Having Other Family Members Who Are Gang Related: It is highly probable that your child will follow suit because of the potential influence one family member has over another. This is especially true with an older family member who will have greater influence over a younger

one. Pay closer attention to their relationship. In fact, it's better to be proactive than reactive. Don't worry about offending. Go ahead and set boundaries making clear what you will and will not tolerate.

10. Bringing up a Child in a Gang Controlled Neighborhood:

You should know that your child is at a greater risk when you live in a gang occupied neighborhood. The majority of black males in my hood joined the "Black Gangster Disciples". Because they controlled the hood, they would either be my tormentors or my guardians. Without real discipline and better role models, I chose the gangster life. Any violations to what's been advised herein, take action without delay.

If you have a child who's been observed imitating these behaviors and questionable practices, you should be greatly concerned and moved to action while you still can. These signs could very well mean your child is definitely gang related, considering joining a gang or is being influenced by gang like behaviors. None of which are good.

Discussion Points The Tell Tale Signs That Your Child Might Be Gang Related

1. Why are parents missing the obvious signs that their child might be gang related?

2. What are some consequences to not seeing these signs?

3. Being in denial that you might have a gang related child, does this do more to help or harm the child? Explain.

4. What does the phrase mean "Once you know better, do better?"

5. Your child seems to favor tough guy villains in films. He's been observed quoting some of the characters' lines. If you were to speak up and object, is this being too controlling? Explain your answer.

6. Why do parents always think their child is the innocent one and that it's the other child who's getting their child into trouble; like influencing them to join a gang when it might be the other way around?

7. Children who are brought up in a gang controlled neighborhood are often judged by where they come from, which is no fault of their own. Should they be looked at any differently than children from more prominent communities?

Liberating A Gang Banger From Gang Bondage

Gangs are represented by a variety of people with different characteristics, beliefs and persuasions; different, yet similar experiences that have led them to where they are in life. I am not a big believer that one solution fits all. It is a combination of things working in harmony to knock some giants down. The sling shooter in David's hand wouldn't have been sufficient alone. The solid rocks he loaded the shooter with played a vital part in the victory David enjoyed over his opponent, Goliath. Here are some carefully compiled incentives to drastically improve the chances of helping to liberate a gang member from gang bondage. They will assist you in penetrating their hardened hearts, making it possible to overcome their barriers of resistance.

1. Prayer: If you are a person of faith. Pray for them to be freed from bondage of the gang. Also, ask God to give you the wisdom and the words to reach them and to open their hearts to the truth.

2. Utilize Humility: Take a soft approach, speak through

kindness. Ask them for their permission to engage in a discussion as to why they have chosen to join a gang.

3. Don't be Judgmental: You do not want them to become defensive. Defensive people are easily offended. They stop listening and go on the defensive, which is counter-productive.

4. Appeal to Reason and Question: If they are willing to talk with you, ask them: since joining a gang, have you received more in return from the gang than what you have given? If they answer they have received more, then ask, what is so valuable that it is worth all you have, including your life? Gangs demand no less from their members. Take time to point out the good things in them that you admire.

5. Be a Good Listener: It's always good to be a good listener. You can learn things about the other person you previously didn't know. Thus, if you're not successful in persuading them this round, in the next round, you'll have even more to work with. Your chances of success will increase.

6. What are Their Religious Beliefs: You want to know whether or not they believe in God? Is there an eternal Heaven and hell? If there is good and evil in the world, on

which side does the gang stand? In standing with the gang, ask them, have you not taken a stand with the devil against God? How will you answer the day you stand before God to give account for your life?

7. The Third Party Approach: There are some hardened, stubborn gang members out there. They will not let you get a word in. The best way to deal with a hardened gang member who refuses to let you speak is through someone the gang member knows and respects. The TPA can be a tremendous asset to you. He or she can be your knight on the board.

8. Appeal to Reason Question: If gangs are everything gang members make them appear to be, what does the gang provide that cannot be obtained outside the gang? The short answer is nothing! Follow up with the question: How are you not being taken advantage of if everything you want and need, can be obtained without all the risk of being in a gang?

9. Build upon Shared Experiences: A way that you can better connect with the gang member is feel free to share any experiences you might have had dealing with gangs; directly or indirectly. Shared experiences build bridges.

10. Patience is a Virtue: Do not despair if the gang member is resistant to your good intentions. He or she can't see the bars that enslave them. You need to open their eyes to the truth. Remember, you are sowing the seed of hope for a better life in them. Every sown seed doesn't sprout and spring up overnight. Some seeds take longer than others to bear fruit. If the sower doesn't sow the good seed, only troublesome weeds, thorns and thickets will grow.

11. Choose not to be Afraid: This is not to say that there should not be a reasonable level of concern when dealing with gang members. Think of this: If everyone remained in their comfort zone, boxed in by fear, there would be no such thing as an ex-gang member. Those who step out and take courage are the ones who make a difference. This fight is not for the faint-hearted, but for the courageous hearted.

12. Be Prepared to Make Certain Sacrifices: The giving of your time is a requirement in winning over gang members. You might have to put other things, equally important, on hold. Be willing to step out of your comfort zone into the danger zone if necessary.

13. Appeal to Reason Question: If the person is African American, use this approach to bring about conviction.

Remind the gang member of the Civil Rights Movement. Ask them how does gang banging, drug dealing, robbery, oppressing other blacks, and murder fit in with Dr. Martin Luther King's dream for a better America and the advancement of black America? How is gang violence helping The Dream to be realized? How is it not hindering The Dream turning it into a nightmare that would have frightened Martin from his sleep? Perhaps this will give them serious consideration about the things they've been doing.

14. Appeal to Reason: Ask African American gang member how black gang members shooting and murdering members of the African American community differs from Klansmen lynching African Americans in the Jim Crow South. Both instances involve the senseless killing of yet another African American.

15. Legacy: Ask gang members what their legacy will be and what they would like for it to reflect. If their response is for a positive legacy, ask how gang banging will help and not prevent their desired legacy.

16. Misguided Goals and Allegiances: Should the gang member express a desire to leave a negative legacy, then the misguided goals and allegiance must be overcome. Ask the gang member why his or her allegiance to the gang greater than that to their biological family, their race or ethnicity, or the rest of the human race. Gang violence and affiliation threaten all of them. The gang member may try to deny his allegiance is misguided. However, their actions speak louder than words. For example, a mother warns her son or daughter not to join a gang, but then the child does what he or she was told not to do. The child's loyalty is not with his or her biological family but with the gang.

17. Have an Exit Plan: Certain Gangs will not simply allow their members to walk away. The gang's strength lies in its numbers. Someone walking away not only subtracts from the gang's numbers but affects the discipline and loyalty to the gang. Furthermore, there is the credo "BLOOD IN BLOOD OUT". For the safety of someone wanting to leave the gang, there should be an exit plan in place. This will give them greater assurance in their departure. Should their life truly be endangered, there is safety in distance, in relocating them to another city for a fresh start. And yes, time away does heal some wounds for those who wish to

return to where they come from someday.

18. Provide Alternatives to Gangs: If someone is willing to walk away from a gang, it will undoubtedly leave a sizable vacancy in their life. That hole has to be filled in quickly, lest they backslide into it. Going from the familiar to the unknown can be frightening. Here are some honorable alternatives: Community college or a four year college, vocational school or the job corps where a trade can be earned. Other options include, the military, a missionary trip to a foreign country where they can be of service to others, employment at a shop or factory so they can earn an income and be productive. All of these and more can occupy one's time, give his or her life purpose of a different kind, and direction as he or she moves forward.

The Unrelenting Burdens of Gang Bangers

Discussion Points
Liberating a Gang Banger
from Gang Bondage

1. If a child was drowning in a lake and you had it in your power to save him or her, would you help? A child is likewise drowning in street gang bondage. It is in your power to help him or her to safety. What kind of person are you if you stand idly by watching him or her drown?

2. Who benefits when a young person walks away from the gang life and takes a different path?

3. What are some positive suggestions to reaching out to gang members that will make them approachable?

4. When dealing with a hardened gang member who refuses to listen to you, what other way should you use? How could you reach a hardened gang member who refuses to talk to you?

5. If you were to appear judgmental and condemning, what's likely to be the response of the gang banger?

6. Can those who fail to do anything toward combating gangs rightly complain when gang violence disrupts the peace of the community?

7. Failure to adequately deal with the gang problems of today, will we not be confronted with an even bigger gang problem tomorrow? Explain your answer.

8. Why would liberating a gang member from gang bondage be worth the sacrifice one may have to make getting them free? Could cases like former gang member Min. Kenneth Williams, the author of "The Unrelenting Burdens of Gang Bangers" and "Liberating a Gang Banger from Gang Bondage", etc., be an excellent example as to why it's worth the time and effort?

Gang Free School Zones: Getting the Gangs Out of Your School and Keeping Them Away

Inner city schools have long been recruitment grounds for gangs targeting young people. Can anyone deny gangs know the location of their bread and meat? Here's the problem which confronts us: Parents are not sending their children off to schools so they can be recruited by gang members on the school grounds or on the way to school, nor leaving it. If kids are going to be recruited, the recruiter should be from a college or the military, not from a gang. Assuming of course, the parents desire the best for their child.

The list below has been specifically prepared to address this problem. It provides a list of suggestions that will counter the gangs' efforts to recruit, reduce their success rate and make matters harder for gangs attempting to operate on or around schools.

1. Draft a zero tolerance gang policy for your school. Insist

that one be written. Copies of the policy should be posted and handed out to teachers, students and be sent out to parents.

2.   All students should be required to read and sign a contract consenting to and adhering to a "Gang Free Zone", while on and around school grounds.

3.   Schools should have a quarterly essay contest on the dangers of gang membership and explain the threat they pose to families, communities, schools, etc. There should be rewards for the top three best written essays, ranging from having their essays published in the local newspaper, read in a school assembly and there should be cash rewards. All other participants should be allowed to have their essays placed on the school's web site. Extra credit should also be rewarded to all participants for encouragement.

4.   Develop an anti-gang program: A class that students can voluntarily take and earn credit, where they can learn about gangs and the threat they pose. A volunteer police officer or school resource officer would teach the class. There should be written assignments dealing with gang activities. Students should be allowed to share aloud their personal

experiences like dealing with gangs in their community. Guest speakers should come and speak with the students, someone who's lived the gang life but left it. Field trips to jails, prisons, cemeteries and morgues should be arranged with the parents' consent. Students can visit with people who have been impacted in some way by gangs. This should be a 30 day program. At its completion, students should receive a certificate of completion signed by their teacher, principal and police chief, if possible. The parents or guardians of the students enrolled within the program should be allowed to join the class, alongside their child around the mid part of the program. Their presence could prove most helpful.

5. Schools should invite reformed ex-gang members to come as guest speakers and share their story at a school assembly. It takes a certain type of person to sometimes reach a certain type of person.

6. Similar to anti-bullying laws, there needs to be anti gang recruitment laws, especially prohibiting gangs from operating on or near schools. School officials should support such a law.

7. Students suspected of being gang related should be warned

that any offense on campus committed by them, deemed to be gang related, it will be mandatory for the student to take the program. A failure to attend and complete the program results in a student must find enrollment elsewhere.

8. Any gang related tattoos must be covered at all times.

    No gang related clothing or wear is permitted on school grounds.

9. School guidance counselors should familiarize themselves with information dealing with gangs and the proper way of dealing with gang related issues. Students should be encouraged to go to them for guidance, and receive the best possible help. In addition, there should be a school hot line where students can call upon counselors for advice for themselves or for others. The caller should have the option to remain anonymous.

10. Make available anti-gang books and literature in the school library.

11. Create an advocacy program that will teach students how to speak out in public against gangs.

    You can't always stop gangs from coming onto school

grounds, whether it is a non-student gang member or an actual student gang member. If the leadership of a school is strong, informed and prepared, and the student body has been well taught, equipped and made ready to meet the threat, as a team, you will not be easily overcome. It is not the habit of gangs to stick around where there's no success. They must feed on new recruits in order to survive and grow. A well planned and executed anti-gang program will reduce the gang activity on your schools campus.

Discussion Points
"Gang Free Zone"

1. What are some benefits to allowing students to compete in an essay contest on the dangers of gang violence and gangs on school grounds?

2. Are zero tolerance gang policies in schools really that necessary? Is the need, if any, being overstated?

3. Do we underestimate our kid's ability to handle gangs that might target them in or around schools?

4. A school that has an actual anti-gang program set up, would this not be an admission that the school has a gang problem or could something better be said of a school that confronts the street gang problem? If so, what?

5. Does parental participation in an anti-gang program increase or decrease the success of an anti-gang program or does it merely distract the kid from learning and being reformed?

6. What does it say about our culture when children sent off to school to get an education have to be cautious against gang

threats?

7. What impact could having anti-gang books in schools, in addition to having a guest speaker at a school assembly to speak out against gang violence, have on students?

GANGS
Getting Them Out and Keeping Them Out of Your Neighborhood

Danger has many faces and the size of the danger is often irrelevant. For example, a tick with an infectious disease can bring death just as certain as a large vicious beast. Nothing should be underestimated, especially when it comes to protecting our families, friends, homes and communities. Prudence dictates that a safety plan be established to guard against all manner of evil. The following recommendations are ways to be proactive in combating gangs:

1. Police Presence: It wards off criminal and gang activities in your neighborhood. It's helpful to have frequent patrols.

2. Neighborhood Watch Program: They are the watchman of the community to warn of impending danger. If there's no one to blow the whistle, how will the community know to arm themselves for battle? A community that unwisely remains unguarded and unprepared risks becoming infected

with a street gang.

3.   Communication: People living in a community should be acquainted with each other on a first name basis. They should have an agreed upon plan in place to protect the community.

4.   Watch Dogs: Barking dogs are a nuisance to gang bangers, criminals and those in the neighborhood who are up to no good. A dog's aggressive barking draws unwanted attention that could lead to the police being called.

5.   Street Lights: A well lit area gives less cover to those who work in the shadows. You can't identify what you don't see. What you can see can be identified, which concerns criminals and gang bangers.

6.   Board Up Vacant Houses: Gang members are known to take cover in vacant houses and buildings with busted out windows and broken down doors. When structures are in disarray, fix them up, board them up or seek to have them scheduled for demolition.

7. Graffiti Free Zone: If there's any graffiti on any structure in your neighborhood, clean it up. It creates a negative

impression on a community. Furthermore, it attracts other gangs to come along with a response to either support or disrespect the previous gang message. This is one way gang members battle.

8. Establish a Respectful Relationship with the Youth in your Community: Kids often know of things that occur within the neighborhood before adults do. They are a great source for information. If they come to respect you, you will have access to a wealth of information

9. Don't hesitate to Call 911: Gang bangers should be made aware that they just can't come into your community and do whatever they want without consequences. They need to know you're not afraid to call the police. Communities that live in fear of gangs rarely call the police even when they themselves are victims. The problem then only festers.

10. Surveillance Cameras: They are a great deterrent to gang activities. A video can be used as evidence in a trial. From a gang bangers perspective, it's best to avoid areas where cameras are mounted.

11. Post signs in your neighborhood like "Neighborhood Watch" don't go unheeded by criminals. They relay a very clear message: "Don't think you're not being watched. "Signs like Gang Free Zone, Drug Free Zone, etc. should

also be posted, making it clear this neighborhood has been claimed. Gangs certainly don't have a problem posting their signs.

12. Be Aware of Potential Hang out Spots: These are places where gang bangers like to gather in alleys, vacant houses or buildings. Once you identify them, keep your children out of these areas. And, make sure other parents know of them. If you can dismantle such a place, after first seeking official approval, don't hesitate to do so.

13. Discontinue Trails and Shortcuts Thru Your Neighborhood if Possible: Trails in the city, in urban areas, are not the same as those in rural suburban areas. These are the trails that run through the neighborhood that draw outsiders, seeking to take a shortcut or stay out of the view of residents. Trails allow people not to be seen on the main roads. Those not wanting to be seen are likely those with something to hide. Gang members and criminals know the trails like the back of their hands.

14. Do Not Profile People: Evil comes in all colors, shapes and sizes. Although the threat is real and bad people are everywhere, there are also a lot of good people around. For the sake of the good, don't jump to conclusions and label

someone visiting your community a gang banger who's up to no good before you can fully investigate. You will only end up creating a problem where there wasn't one. Learn not to judge a book by its cover. Be a wise observer of good and evil.

"In order to get one thing out, you only need to flood it with another. The good pushes the bad out, as does light to darkness." Kenneth D. Williams

Either communities will rise up against gangs and take back what's theirs or stay down in defeat of an opponent who's only as strong as we allow.

The Unrelenting Burdens of Gang Bangers

Discussion Points
Gangs-Getting Them Out and Keeping Them Out of Your Neighborhood

1. The phrase "It only takes one person to get the ball rolling", can this principle also apply in one person's determination to rid his or her neighborhood of gangs? Is the power and presence of a gang too much for one person to make an impact?

2. Is a street gang more or less likely to establish roots in a community that has a neighborhood watch program? Why or why not?

3. What are some ways that you can identify a hang out spot for gang members in your community? Does the spot always have to look the same?

4. Why is it so important to establish communication with others living in your community? What are some dangers for not doing so?

5. How can children and teens in your community be of use against a street gang moving into your area?

6. Is a well lit area a deterrent to crime? Explain.

7. Why is it better to be proactive than reactive when dealing with street gangs?

The Gangster Disciples' Unholy Book of Life

Neither I, nor anyone else I know ever saw the mythological "Book of Life" The Gangster Disciples are taught that exists for their names to be inscribed in. Nonetheless, it was no less real to me and plenty of other misguided disciples. Only the True Blue Gangsters were to have their names written in it. Striving for this reward was my everything. It was to be obtained the hard way, in the streets where anything goes.

This so called "Book of Life" is not to be confused with the Lamb's (Jesus Christ) Book of Life in Heaven, wherein the names of the Saints of God are written.

The Gangs' Book of Life has all the appearance of greatness and is thought to be something to be desired. However, it only offers death and ruin to those whose names are written. But of course, this truth would be concealed. Only the lie revealed or else no one would desire it.

The street gangs' "Book of Life" is an unholy one by definition, no one's name is written in it for the good they do, only for the bad. Doing evil doesn't lead to life; it leads to death. Any name that's been written in this book has been done so in blood. The blood of their victims cries out to God for justice that He will not ignore.

The author of this "Unholy Book of Life" comes to kill, steal and to destroy. Do not let him (Satan) seduce you into believing his lies. If you are a person whose name has been written in this book, have hope. It can be unwritten with the help of Almighty God. With Him, all things are possible. It can also be unwritten if you settle it in your heart and allow yourself to be moved to action with the help of true friends.

The Street Gangs' Kiss of Death

There's this quote gang superiors like to use to influence and entice subordinate members. They say "Getting down for your crown". This wasn't a literal crown, but a figurative one. Not to be worn on your head but around the heart where pride is stored up; lifting you up, having you thinking you're bigger than you really are. Recipients of this crown get bragging rights for their lawless deeds...For better or for worse, they've made a name for themselves recognized in the streets. All this only serves to make a person a target for some other rival gang member trying to make a name for him or herself. What you thought was intended to promote you actually demotes you, through making you a target. It's no more than betrayal, sealed with a "crown of a kiss".

"Getting down for your crown" brings about ruin. Anything to be had in the short run, you lose even more in the long run.

This is the type of kiss you shun away from. This is the type of kiss no human being should be trying to give another. And it has been known to back-fire on the one attempting to give it.

Judas Iscariot, he betrayed Jesus Christ with a kiss and learned this truth the hard way: in death.

Those who seek after a crown and a kiss that's given in love, there's the crown of life, available for you in Heaven. Once you have it, no one can take it from you! It neither rusts, rots or fades away. The kisses up there are to "LIVE FOR" Forever!

The Street Gang's Distorted Rite-of-Passage

In early Native American culture, young men entering into adulthood did so through an intense rite-of-passage unique to his tribe. This transition and tradition was passed down from their ancestors requiring participants to prove their tribal worth.

Courage was an absolute requirement. In order to be received into manhood this glorious courage was seen in young braves racing out on horseback to bring down the great and mighty buffalo, which could instantly kill with one swipe of its deadly horns, or kick from its bone crushing rock hard hoofs. This courage was seen in braves attacking their enemies who threaten their land and hunting grounds. It was in the completion of a vision quest, which tested their soul, body and spirit. They were tried and tested by the fire. Only the brave at heart survived. Those counted worthy were held in high esteem by the tribe. They became warriors who earned the right to be seated at the council of fire among the elders. The Native Americans rite-of-passages are honorable and worthy of note. However, not all rites-of-passage are honorable and worthy of note. Some rites-of-passage do not cultivate virtue, but rather pollute and corrupt our youth, leaving a path of destruction in its wake.

These troublesome perpetrators are criminal street gangs of whom I speak. They entice, and in some cases, order potential members to commit hideous and violent crimes to prove their loyalty to the gang; to prove they have heart (translated; guts or courage). It is cowardice not courage that preys on the weak. A further descent into degradation: imprisonment for one's crimes, for carrying out the gang's affairs. This results in promotion of status. But you must pass the test of keeping your mouth shut. Don't be a snitch. Also, you must not allow yourself to be treated like a weakling on the inside. Street creds were the big reward for those who kept to the code.

Street gangs are exploiting and taking advantage of the weaknesses of others. Many young African American and Hispanic males have fallen hard into this trap. They have been too blind to discern the truth. Gangs are stealing their future right from beneath them, leaving them thinking they're receiving something special and exceptional in exchange.

They get a criminal record that follows them wherever they go. This makes certain employment opportunities and clearances impossible.

Regarding courage, the gang's rite-of passage distorts the true meaning of it. Courage entails mental and moral strength to venture, persevere, and withstand danger, fear or difficulty (of an honorable sort).

Morals entail: Noble means conforming to a standard of what is right and good. There's nothing good, right, noble or moral about a rite-of-passage that requires a person to cause unjustifiable harm to himselves or others.

People would be better off not taking part in a street gang's rite-of-passage. They only stand to lose more than they gain. And of course, certain things that are gained are what you wish you had not obtained.

Discussion Points
The Street Gangs'
Distorted Rite-of-Passage

1. What was the intended purpose of the rite-of-passage?

2. How is the true meaning and purpose of the Rite-of-Passage being distorted by street gangs?

3. Can you think of some worthy and honorable rites-of-passage?

4. What are some dishonorable rites-of-passage you might know about?

5. Why would people knowingly participate in a rite-of-passage they know is not legitimate?

6. In what ways can we as a society, guard against assaults on the integrity and genuineness of our rites-of-passage?

7. Have you ever participated in a rite-of-passage? If you answered yes, if you could add or take away something about the experience, what would it be and why?

Testimony

You have no idea what this book did too me or for me. My mother wrote me a letter last week saying a prophet of God is in my mist and will reveal himself soon I really am having a hard time surrendering myself to God, because like you said in your book, we cant serve two masters and we both know that's not possible. Thank you for your message and story. Once I calm down I'll get at you, let me soak all this in.

Prisoner: Marcus Adkins
B.K.A Big Cuz

Marcus would later ask me to lead him in to a relationship with Jesus Christ.

Min. Kenneth Williams

The Unrelenting Burdens of Gang Bangers

Support the effort to make the "Neutral of Gangs", N.O.G. symbol, a global and officially recognized anti-gang symbol.

Minister Kenneth Williams
SK-000957
P. O. Box 400 VSM
Grady, AR   71644
USA

The Unrelenting Burdens of Gang Bangers

Conclusion

The Bible says there's only one way to Heaven!

> *"Jesus said "I am the way, the truth, and the life: no man cometh unto the Father, but by me."* John 14:6

> NOBODY ELSE CAN SAVE YOU.
> TRUST JESUS TODAY!

> *"That if thou shalt confess with thy mouth the Lord Jesus, and shalt believe in thine heart that God hath raised him from the dead, thou shalt be saved."* Romans 10:9

1. Admit you are a sinner. See Romans 3:10

2. Be willing to turn from sin (repent): see Acts 17:30

3. Believe that Jesus Christ died for you, was buried and rose from the dead. See Romans 10:9-10

Through prayer, invite Jesus into your life to become your personal savior. See Romans 10:13

What to Pray

Dear God, I am a sinner and need forgiveness. I believe that Jesus Christ shed His precious blood and died for my sin. I am willing to turn from sin. I now invite Christ to come into my heart and life as my personal savior.

If you trusted Jesus as your savior, you have just begun a wonderful new life with him.

Now,

1. Read your Bible (KJV) every day to get to know Jesus Christ better.

2. Talk to God in prayer every day.

3. Be baptized, worship, fellowship, and serve with other Christians in church where Christ is preached and the Bible is the final authority.

4. Tell others about Jesus Christ

The Unrelenting Burdens of Gang Bangers

About the Author

Williams, Kenneth

SK# 957

Kenneth Williams is certainly not a man without his fair share of faults. Growing up, he was a stiff neck riff-raff hell-bent on learning the hard way, as if it was the only way. His choice to join the Black Gangster Disciples at nine years old, sure enough further aggravated matters for him. What would you say about a 10-year-old being locked up in the boy's reformatory school back-to-back. That was Kenneth.

At 16, he served his first prison sentence. Kenneth was released at 19 years old, on April 02, 1998. His freedom, if it could be called that, lasted eight months, a period during which he got innocent blood all over his hands. Rightfully so, Kenneth has not seen the light of day since, as the saying goes.

Notwithstanding, what the devil meant for evil, God can turn it around for our good. Although Kenneth remains on Arkansas's death row, he says that he is freer within than he's ever been, thanks to the one who holds the master keys to any prison, to any infirmary: the Lord Jesus Christ.

He has no greater joy than sharing his testimony of how God delivered him from darkness.

Kenneth is an anti-gang advocate. He is the founder of a nonprofit organization in the making – he calls it N.O.G. for Neutral Of Gangs, initiative.

He is an ordained minister of the gospel of Jesus Christ with First Trinity C.O.G.I.C., located in Pine Bluff, Arkansas. USA.

www.ingramcontent.com/pod-product-compliance
Lightning Source LLC
Chambersburg PA
CBHW072059280526
45788CB00006B/2328